Learn To Play
Electric Guitar
The Complete Method For The Beginner Guitarist

By

Paul Andrews & Alan Garrett

Welcome to *Learn To Play Electric Guitar*. This book is designed to give beginners a solid foundation in electric guitar playing techniques such as Power Chords, Open Chords, Barre Chords and various Lead Guitar Techniques.

Once completed, you will be ready to study any genre that takes your fancy, be it Rock, Metal, Blues, Jazz, Acoustic, Alternative etc.

 Visit www.6stringbooks.com/ltpeg to download the book's accompanying audio.

CREDITS

All tracks recorded at *Ardent Studios*, Deal, 2010, 2012 & 2015

All songs written, recorded and produced by **Paul Andrews** & **Alan Garrett**

Tracks 20, 21, 24 & 25 Piano by **Brian Orwell**

ISBN-13: 978-1481270557

ISBN-10: 1481270559

STRING BOOKS

Copyright © 2015 by 6 String Books

International Copyright Secured   All Rights Reserved

No part of this publication may be reproduced in any form or by any means without the prior written permission of the publisher

www.6stringbooks.com

CONTENTS

INTRODUCTION — 1
- GUITAR PARTS — 1
- STRING NAMES — 1
- CHORD BOXES — 2
- SCALE BOXES — 3
- TABLATURE — 3
- STANDARD NOTATION — 4

CHAPTER 1 OPEN POWER CHORDS — 7
- RHYTHM — 7
- OPEN POWER CHORDS SONG ONE — 10
- PICKED POWER CHORDS — 12
- OPEN POWER CHORDS SONG TWO — 13

CHAPTER 2 12 BAR BLUES — 15
- EIGHTH NOTES — 15
- BLUES CHORD PATTERN — 16
- 12 BAR BLUES SONG ONE — 17
- SHUFFLE RHYTHM — 19
- 12 BAR BLUES SONG TWO — 21

CHAPTER 3 MINOR PENTATONIC OPEN POSITION — 22
- 'A' MINOR PENTATONIC SCALE — 22
- RIFF ONE — 23
- 'E' MINOR PENTATONIC SCALE — 24
- RIFF TWO — 25

CHAPTER 4 IMPROVISATION — 26
- 'A' MINOR PENTATONIC LICKS — 26
- SOLO ONE — 29
- 'E' MINOR PENTATONIC LICKS — 30
- SOLO TWO — 32

CHAPTER 5 OPEN CHORDS — 33
- MAJOR CHORDS — 33
- MINOR CHORDS — 34
- CHORD CHANGING — 35
- OPEN CHORDS SONG ONE — 36
- OPEN CHORDS SONG TWO — 38

CHAPTER 6 MOVABLE POWER CHORDS — 40

- 6ᵀᴴ STRING ROOT POWER CHORDS — 40
- POWER CHORDS SONG ONE — 42
- 5ᵀᴴ STRING ROOT POWER CHORDS — 43
- POWER CHORDS SONG TWO — 45
- MIXED STRING POWER CHORDS — 47
- PALM MUTING — 48
- POWER CHORDS SONG THREE — 49

CHAPTER 7 HALF BARRE CHORDS — 50

- HALF BARRE CHORDS — 50
- HALF BARRE CHORDS SONG ONE — 53
- HALF BARRE CHORDS SONG TWO — 55

CHAPTER 8 BARRE CHORDS — 57

- 6ᵀᴴ STRING BARRE CHORDS — 57
- BARRE CHORDS SONG ONE — 59
- 5ᵀᴴ STRING BARRE CHORDS — 61
- BARRE CHORDS SONG TWO — 63
- MIXED STRING BARRE CHORDS — 64
- SIXTEENTH NOTES — 66
- BARRE CHORDS SONG THREE — 67

CHAPTER 9 LEAD GUITAR — 69

- MOVABLE MINOR PENTATONIC SCALE — 69
- ALTERNATE PICKING — 70
- STRING BENDING — 70
- HAMMER-ONS — 72
- PULL-OFFS — 73
- SLIDES — 74
- SOLO STUDY — 75

LISTENING — 76

LEGEND — 77

- LEAD GUITAR TECHNIQUES — 77
- FINGER PICKING — 78
- PLECTRUM PICKING — 78
- GENERAL NOTATION — 78
- REPEATS — 79
- DYNAMICS — 81
- GENERAL MUSICAL TERMS — 81

INTRODUCTION

GUITAR ANATOMY

The guitar can be divided into three main parts—the body, neck and head—with each part containing numerous elements (shown in the illustration below). Stretching across all three parts of the guitar are the six strings, which are used to create the instrument's sound.

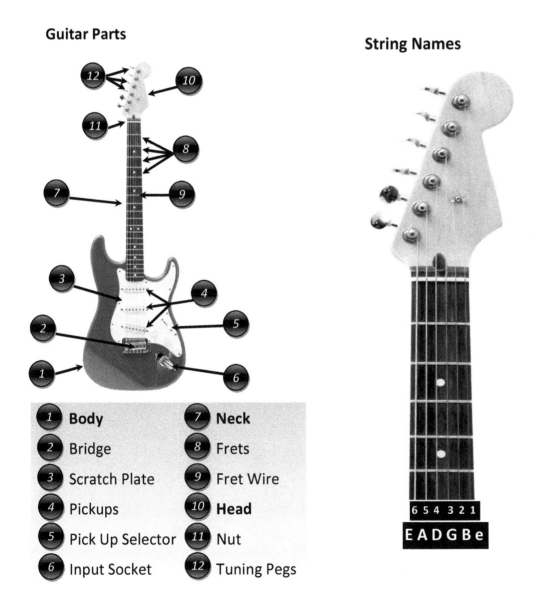

Guitar Parts

1. Body
2. Bridge
3. Scratch Plate
4. Pickups
5. Pick Up Selector
6. Input Socket
7. Neck
8. Frets
9. Fret Wire
10. Head
11. Nut
12. Tuning Pegs

String Names

6 5 4 3 2 1
E A D G B e

Chord Boxes

Chord boxes are graphical representations of the guitar neck used to demonstrate chords. The vertical lines represent the six strings of the guitar and the horizontal lines represent the strips of metal that divide the neck into frets.

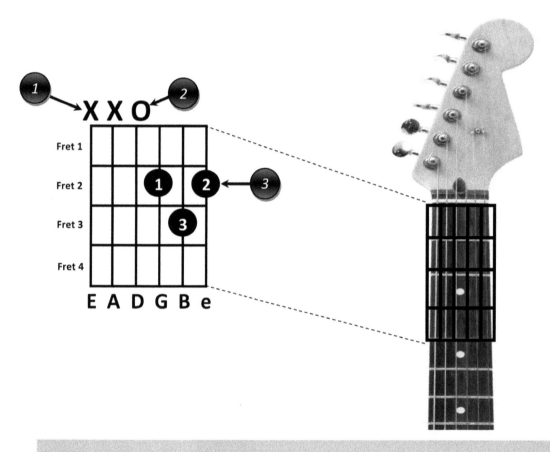

1. The '**X**' above a string indicates which string or strings should not be played.

2. The '**O**' above a string indicates an open string. An open string is performed by playing a string but not holding it down along the guitar neck.

3. The black circles indicate where to place the fingers along the guitar neck. The numbers within the circles indicate which fingers to use, i.e. 1 = index finger, 2 = middle finger, 3 = ring finger & 4 = little finger

Scale Boxes

Scale boxes are used to notate scales, but, unlike chord boxes, the dots are to be played one at a time, starting at the bottom (thickest string) and moving from left to right.

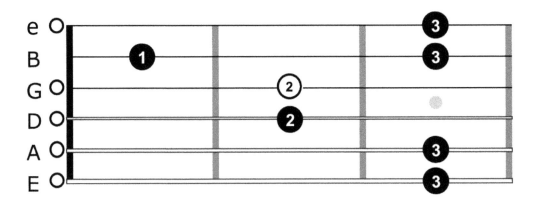

Tablature

Tablature (or Tab for short) is one of the most common systems of notating guitar music. Tab consists of six lines with each line representing one of the six strings on the guitar.

Tablature is always written with the strings upside down, the thickest string (string 6 or E) is represented as the bottom line and the thinnest string (string 1) is represented as the top line.

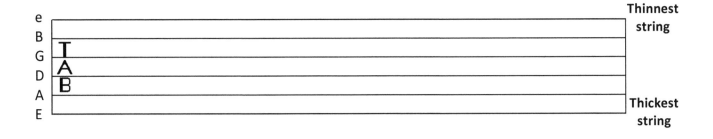

Numbers are placed on top of the lines to indicate which fret to play on that particular string. A '0' represents an open string, meaning you play the string without holding it down with the left hand. A '2' on a line would indicate to hold down fret '2' on that particular string. When numbers are stacked on top of one another this means play them all together.

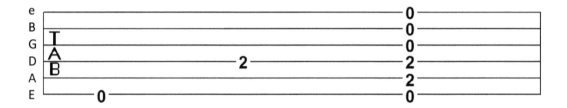

Standard Notation

Standard notation is the traditional system used to notate music. Unlike tablature, standard notation is used by all instruments, not just guitar. Often, tablature and standard notation are grouped together, as shown below.

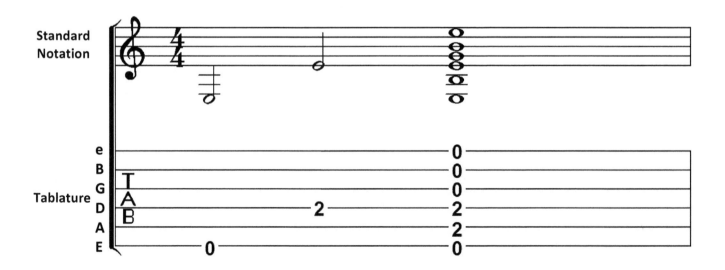

Vertical lines, known as bar lines, are used to divide the music into bars, making it easier to read.

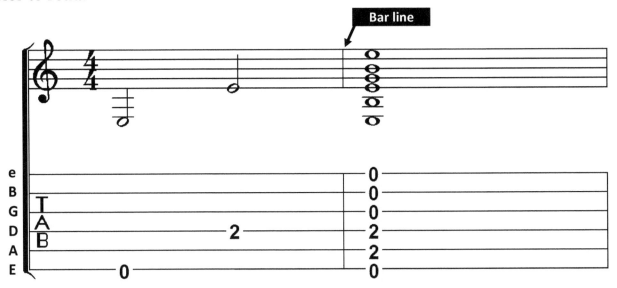

Two thin bar lines are used to mark the end of a section in a piece of music.

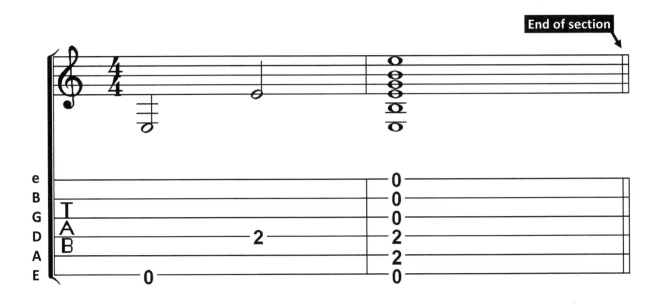

A final bar line is a thin line followed by a thick line, which indicates the end of a piece of music.

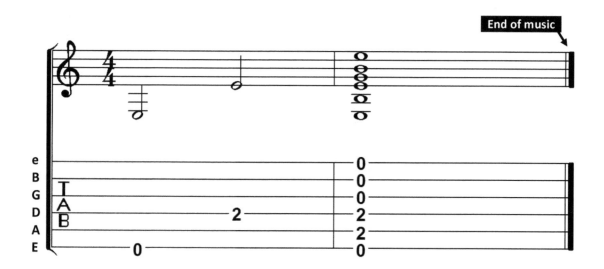

A final bar line with two dots is a repeat sign. A repeat sign is placed at the beginning and end of a section of music to indicate that it should be repeated.

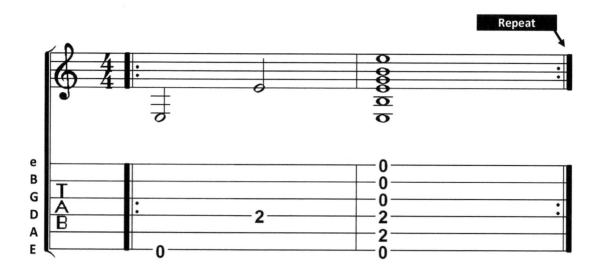

CHAPTER 1 OPEN POWER CHORDS

Power chords are found extensively in rock, pop, blues and metal. They are one of the easiest chord types to play on the guitar as you only need to use one finger, as demonstrated in Ex.1a.

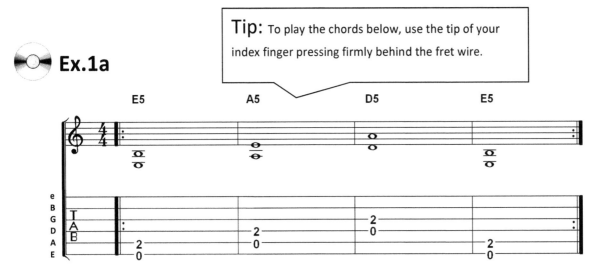

Rhythm

Music is made up of two elements; pitch and rhythm. Pitch refers to the notes you play and rhythm is how long you play them for.

The whole note indicates a note that lasts for four counts, or an entire bar. This simply means you play and count to four, as demonstrated below.

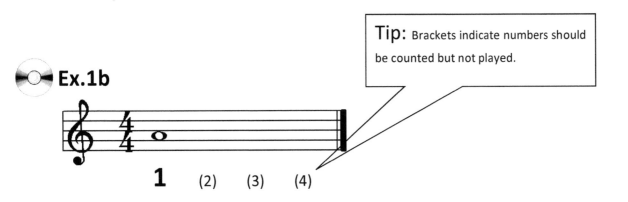

The half note rings out for two counts and lasts for half the bar; this simply means you play and count to two.

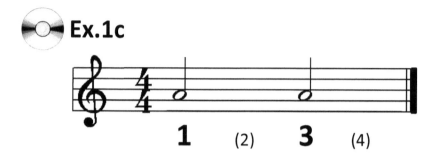

Ex.1c

The quarter note rings out for one count and lasts for a quarter of the bar.

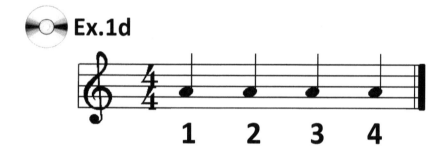

Ex.1d

Symbol	Name	Value
o	Whole note	4 Counts (one to a bar)
♩ (half)	Half note	2 Counts (two to a bar)
♩	Quarter note	1 Count (four to a bar)

The exercises below combine the whole, half and quarter note rhythms with the three power chords covered in Ex.1a.

Tip: This symbol (:||) is called a Repeat. The Repeat symbol is placed at the start and end of a section, which indicates it is to be repeated.

Ex.1e

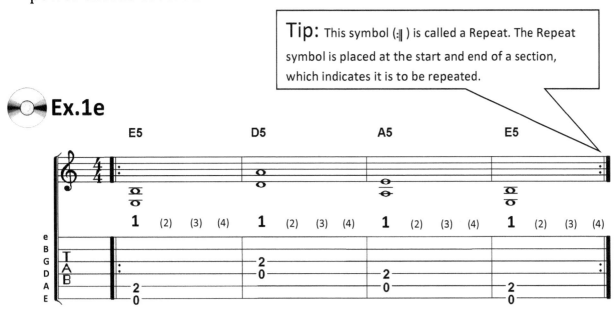

Ex.1f

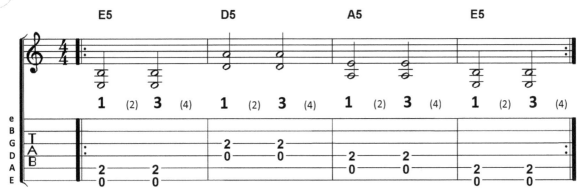

Ex.1g

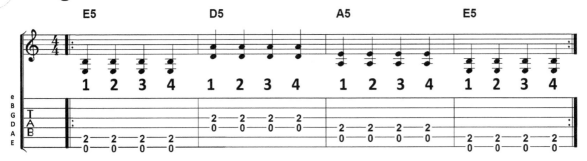

Open Power Chords Song One

The following piece is in the style of AC/DC and combines all of the topics covered so far.

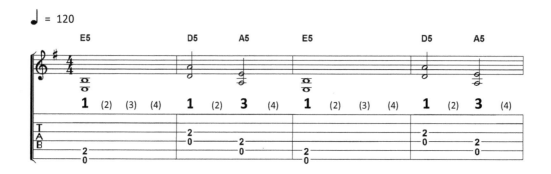

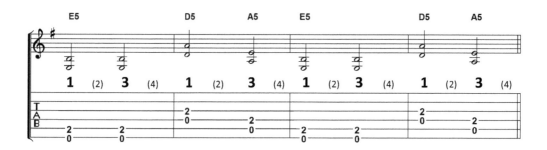

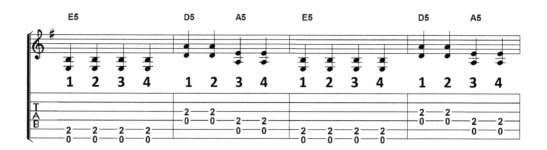

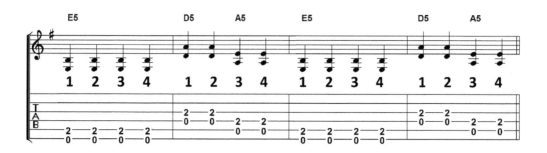

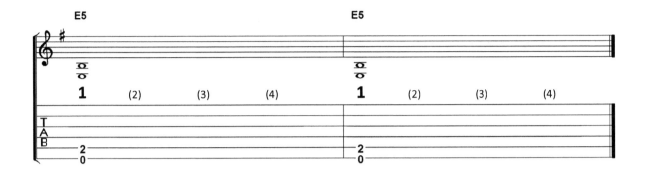

Further Listening:

- **AC/DC** "Highway to Hell", "Back in Black"
- **Bryan Adams** "Summer of 69"
- **Nirvana** "Lithium"

When playing power chords, both strings do not always have to be played together; they can be played/picked separately. This approach is demonstrated below.

 Ex.1h

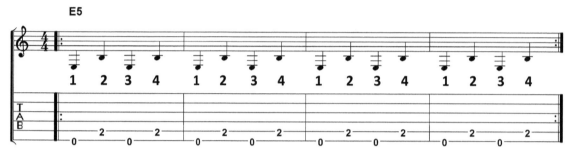

> Tip: *x4* is an instruction to repeat the section four times in total.

 Ex.1i

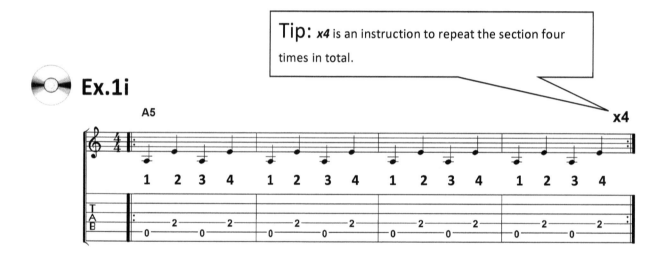

Ex.1j

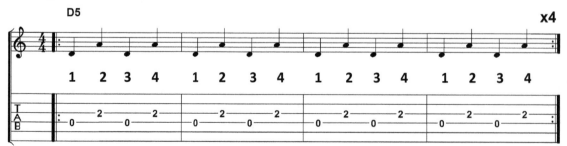

Open Power Chords Song Two

The following piece is in the style of contemporary artists such as Coldplay and Snow Patrol.

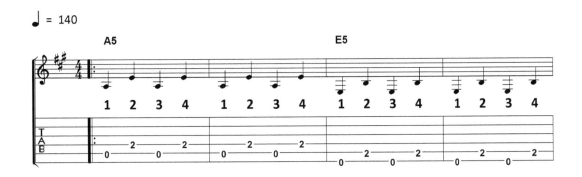

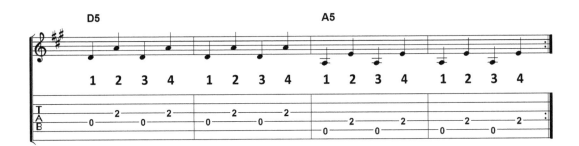

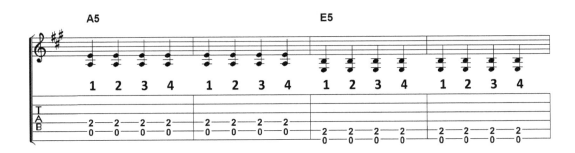

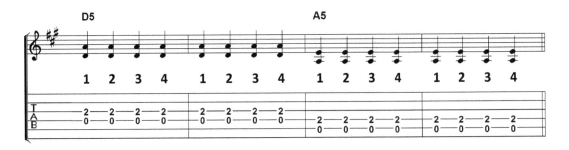

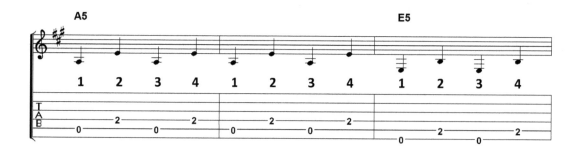

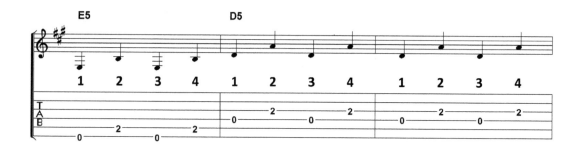

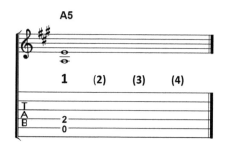

Further Listening:

- **Snow Patrol** "Chasing Cars", "Run"
- **Coldplay** "In My Place"
- **Travis** "Driftwood"

CHAPTER 2   12 BAR BLUES

The 12 bar blues is the most common chord progression found in contemporary music such as blues, rock and roll, and jazz. The progression consists of three chords played over 12 bars.

Eighth Notes

The eighth note is played for half a count and lasts for an eighth of a bar; this simply means you play twice for each count, as demonstrated below.

 Ex.2a

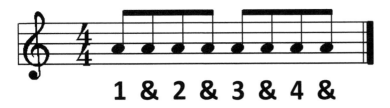

1 & 2 & 3 & 4 &

> **Tip:** Rests indicate a break in a piece of music. For every note there is an equivalent rest. When a rest is present, make sure to stop all strings so there is complete silence.

Notes	Rests	Name	Value
𝕠	▬	Whole note	4 Counts (one to a bar)
𝅗𝅥	▬	Half note	2 Counts (two to a bar)
♩	𝄽	Quarter note	1 Count (four to a bar)
♪	𝄾	Eighth note	½ Count (eight to a bar)

– 15 –

The exercises below take the power chords from Chapter One and add the third finger on the fourth fret to create a typical blues chord pattern.

Ex.2b

Tip: Ensure you only strum two strings, taking care not to hit the remaining four.

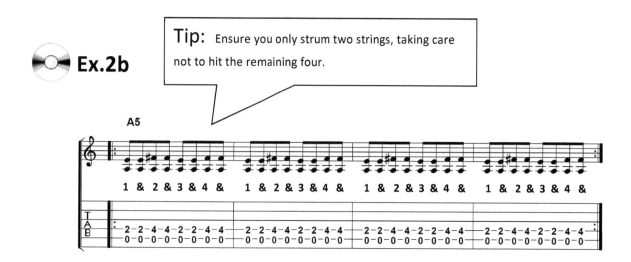

Ex.2c

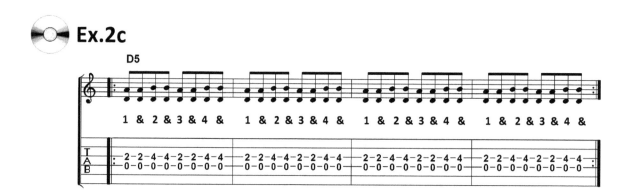

Ex.2d

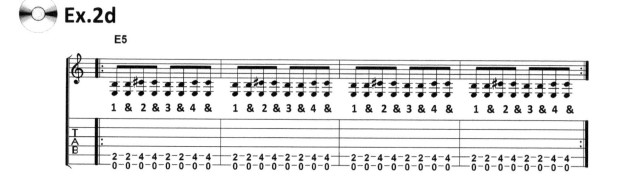

12 Bar Blues Song One

The following example is a 50's rock and roll piece in the style of Chuck Berry.

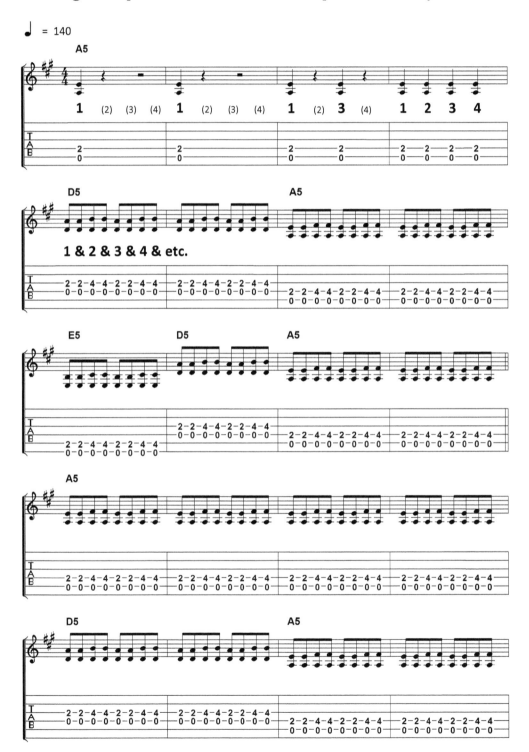

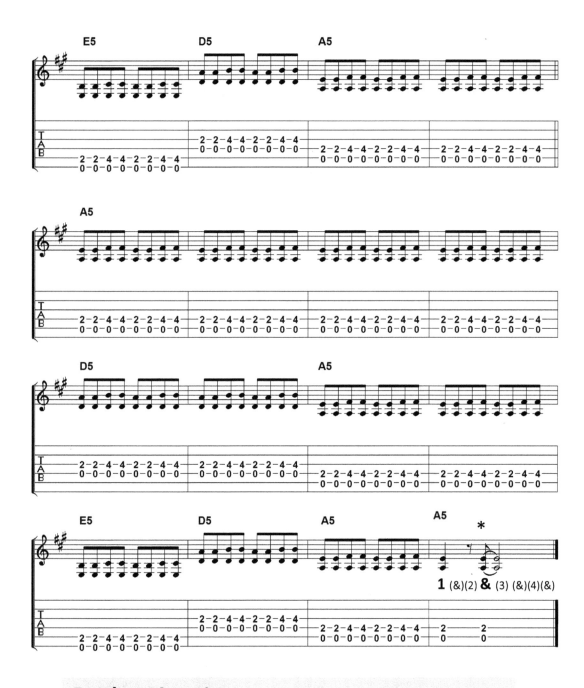

Further Listening:

- **Chuck Berry** "Johnny B. Goode", "Roll Over Beethoven"
- **Stevie Ray Vaughan** "Look at Little Sister"
- **John Mayer** "Route 66"

*Tip: This symbol (⌣) indicates a Tie. A Tie is an arched line connecting two notes of the same pitch, indicating that they are to be played as a single note with their values/counts combined.

Shuffle Rhythm

The shuffle rhythm appears frequently in blues, rock and jazz. It is based on a pair of eighth notes where the first eighth note is held twice as long as the second. This gives the rhythm a 'bounce' or 'lazy' feel.

The easiest way to think of and play a shuffle rhythm is to first divide a beat into three equal parts:

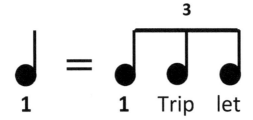

When a note is divided into three equal parts it is called a triplet and has a three displayed above it. The three eighth notes in the above triplet are played in the same time it would normally take to play two eighth notes.

To create a shuffle rhythm, tie the first and the second eighth notes of the triplet together, as this makes the first eighth note twice as long as the third, as shown below:

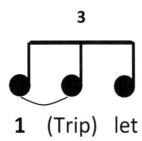

The exercises below demonstrate the difference between playing eighth notes with a straight feel and playing them with a shuffle feel.

Ex.2e (straight)

Tip: This symbol (♪=♪) indicates that all the eighth notes in the piece are to be played with a shuffle rhythm.

 Ex.2f (shuffle)

♪ = ♪♪

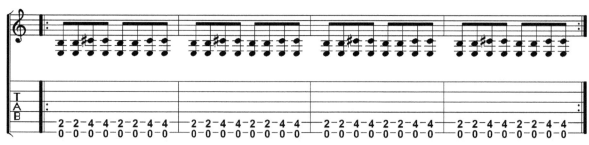

12 Bar Blues Song Two

The following song is a slow blues in the style of T-Bone Walker. The piece is a quick change blues, which simply means you change to the 'D' chord in bar two.

Further Listening:

- **T-Bone Walker** "Stormy Monday Blues"
- **Eric Clapton** "Have You Ever Loved a Woman"
- **B.B. King** "Sweet Sixteen"

*Tip: The bar marked **1** is played the first time through the piece but omitted on the repeat and replaced with the bar marked **2**.

CHAPTER 3   MINOR PENTATONIC OPEN POSITION

The minor pentatonic scale is the most widely used scale in rock and pop guitar. This scale has been used in some of the most memorable guitar riffs and solos of all time such as Eric Clapton's "Layla", Rage Against the Machine's "Bombtrack" and Lenny Kravitz's "Are you Gonna Go My Way".

The example below demonstrates the A minor pentatonic scale played using open and fretted notes.

A Minor Pentatonic Scale

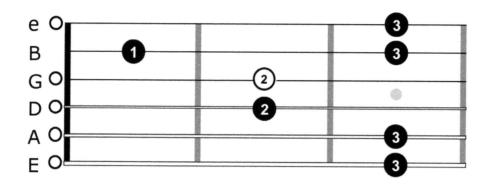

 Ex.3a

Technique Focus
✓ Use the same finger number as fret number e.g. third finger in fret 3
✓ Play all notes at the same speed taking care not to speed up or slow down

Riff One

The following musical phrase uses the A minor pentatonic scale to create a riff in the style of The Killers.

Further Listening:

- **The Killers** "Smile Like You Mean It"
- **Block Party** "I Still Remember"
- **Led Zeppelin** "Immigrant Song"

The example below demonstrates the E minor pentatonic scale played using open and fretted notes.

E Minor Pentatonic Scale

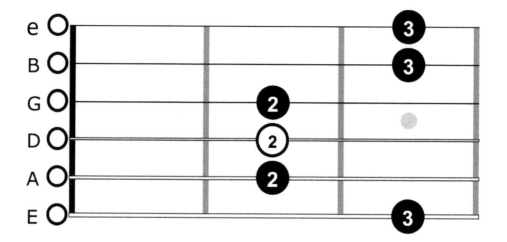

 Ex.3b

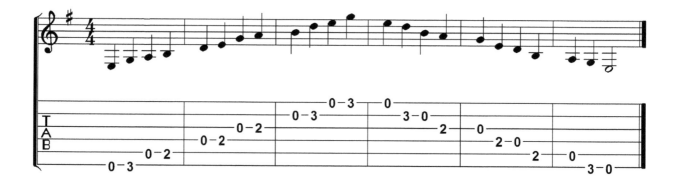

Riff Two

Riff two uses the E minor pentatonic scale to create a riff in the style of Rage Against The Machine.

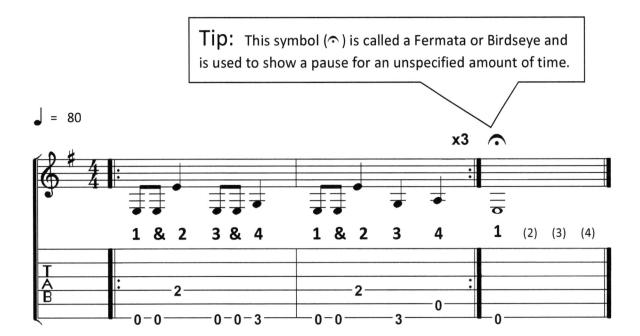

Further Listening:

- **Audioslave** "Cochise"
- **Lenny Kravitz** "Are You Gonna Go My Way"
- **The Beatles** "Day Tripper"

CHAPTER 4   IMPROVISATION

Improvisation can be intimidating to the beginner guitarist as it is often perceived as making up complete solos on-the-spot. In actual fact, improvisation is a process of reorganising pre-learned musical phrases (licks) to create new ideas.

Below are a series of licks that will later be used as building blocks for a solo.

 Ex.4a

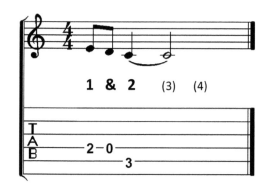

 Ex.4b

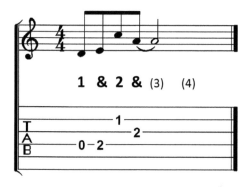

Ex.4c

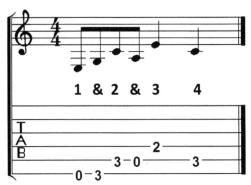

 Ex.4d

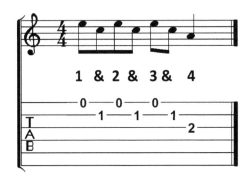

 Ex.4e

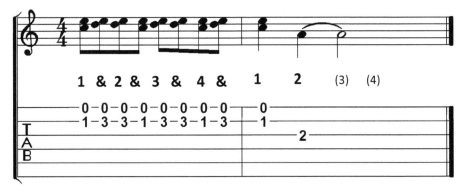

Ex.4f

Ex.4g

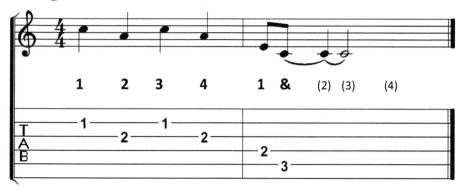

Solo One

Solo one demonstrates the pre-learned licks and how they can be incorporated into an improvised solo. Once you have mastered the solo, try reorganising the licks to create your own solo over the backing track.

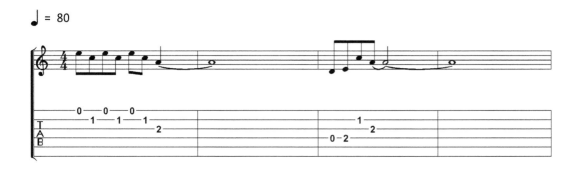

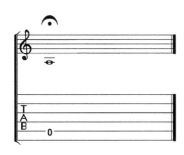

Further Listening:

- **Joe Bonamassa** "Ballad Of John Henry"
- **Led Zeppelin** "Black Dog"
- **Jimi Hendrix** "Purple Haze"

The following licks are taken from the E minor pentatonic scale, shown in Ex.3b, and will be incorporated into the next solo.

 Ex.4h

 Ex.4i

 Ex.4j

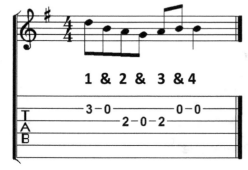

Ex.4k

 ### Ex.4l

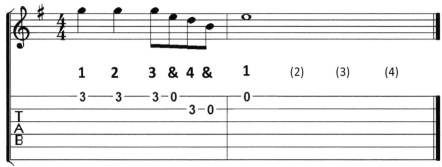

 ### Ex.4m

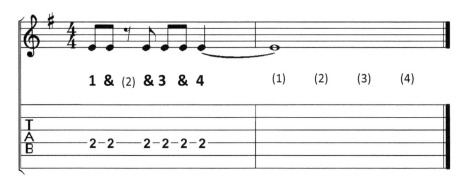

Solo Two

The second solo in this chapter combines the pre-learned E minor pentatonic licks into a funk solo.

Further Listening:

- **Wild Cherry** "Play That Funky Music"
- **Stevie Wonder** "Superstition"
- **The Red Hot Chili Peppers** "Suck My Kiss"

CHAPTER 5 OPEN CHORDS

In this chapter we will be expanding our chord knowledge through the use of open chords. As the name suggests, these chords utilize open strings and the first three frets of the guitar.

There are two main types of open chords; major and minor. The major chord has a happy/bright sound compared to the minor's sad/dark sound.

Major Chords

Tip: O = String is played 'open' with no finger pressed on it
X = Do not play string

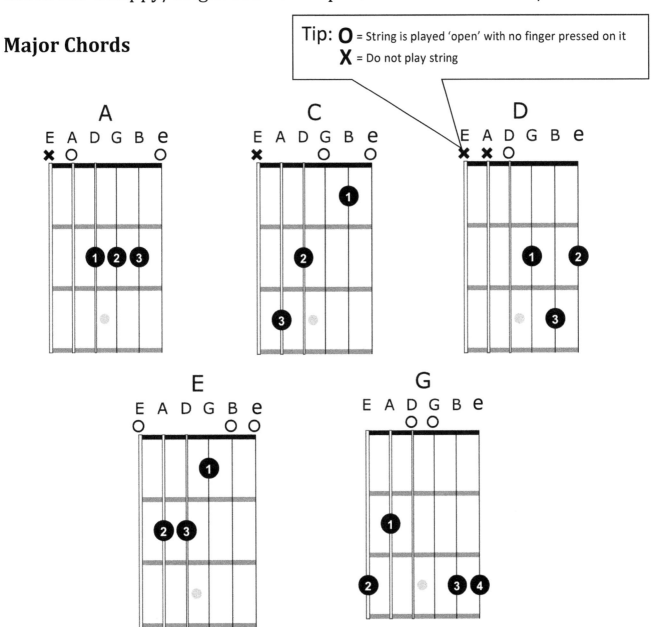

Major Chords

> **Tip:** The small 'm' after the capital letter indicates a minor chord.
> Am = A Minor
> A = A Major

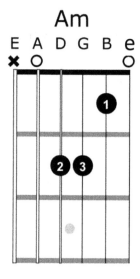
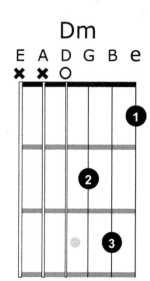
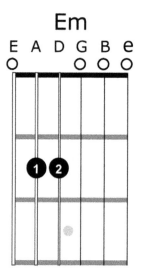

Technique Focus

- ✓ Use the tips of your fretting-hand fingers when pressing down on a string
- ✓ Position fingertips close to the fret wire
- ✓ Keep all fingers arched, taking care not to touch adjacent strings

Chord Changing

When changing between chords there are a few techniques we can employ to make the changes more fluent and accurate; one such technique is the use of common tones.

Common tones are notes that are common to neighbouring chords in a chord progression, such as the boxed notes in Ex.5a and Ex.5b.

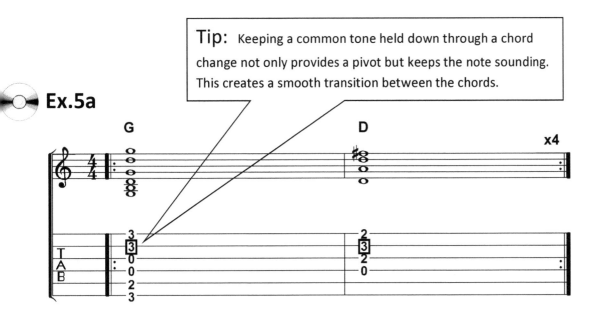

Tip: Keeping a common tone held down through a chord change not only provides a pivot but keeps the note sounding. This creates a smooth transition between the chords.

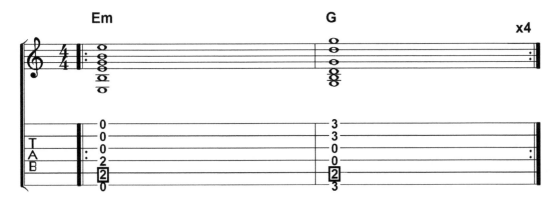

Open Chords Song One

The next song is a modern alternative rock piece in the style of Josh Rouse. The piece uses the following chords; G, D, A and Em.

 = 140

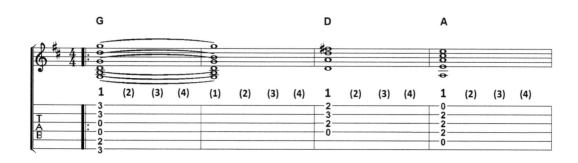

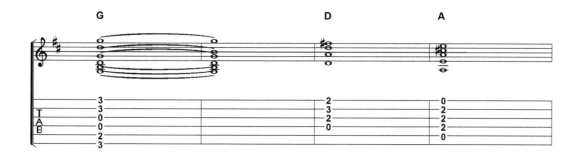

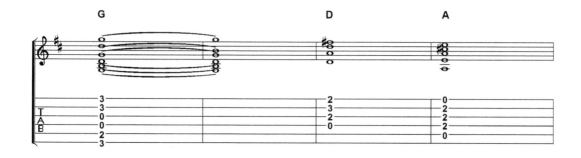

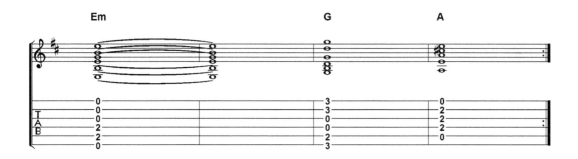

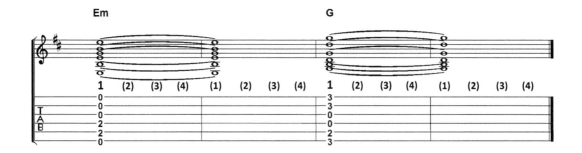

Further Listening:

- **Ryan Adams** "So Alive"
- **Bruce Springsteen** "Working on a Dream"
- **The Goo Goo Dolls** "Slide"

Open Chords Song Two

The following is a hard rock piece in the style of Guns 'N' Roses.

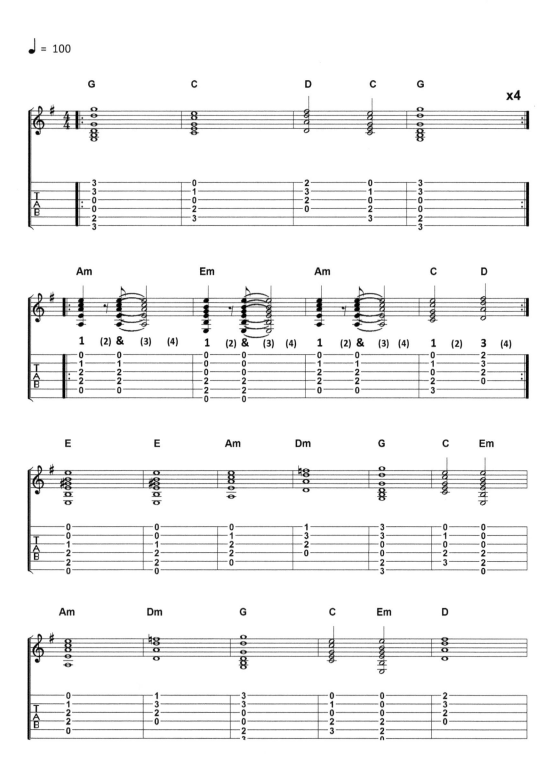

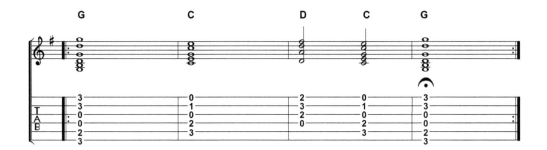

Further Listening:

- **Guns 'N' Roses** "Paradise City"
- **Aerosmith** "I Don't Want To Miss a Thing"
- **The Eagles** "Tequila Sunrise"

CHAPTER 6   MOVABLE POWER CHORDS

In this chapter we will begin to explore the guitar neck beyond the first three frets using movable power chords.

Power chords can be found in many classic guitar riffs such as The Kinks' "You Really Got me", Black Sabbath's "Iron Man", Survivor's "Eye of the Tiger" and Nirvana's "Smells like Teen Spirit".

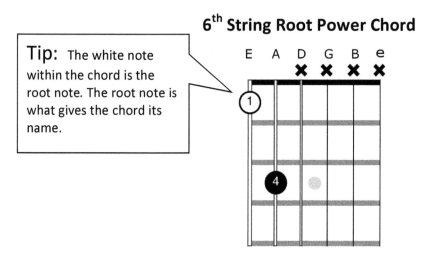

Notes Along the Bottom E String

The diagram below shows the notes along the length of the low E string. To play a particular chord we need to ensure that the root note is in the correct fret, e.g. for a G5 power chord place the root note (finger one) at the third fret.

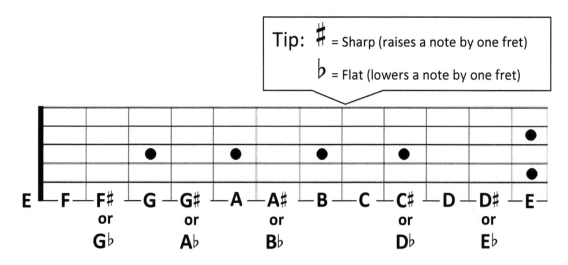

The exercises below utilize the 6th string root power chords along the neck.

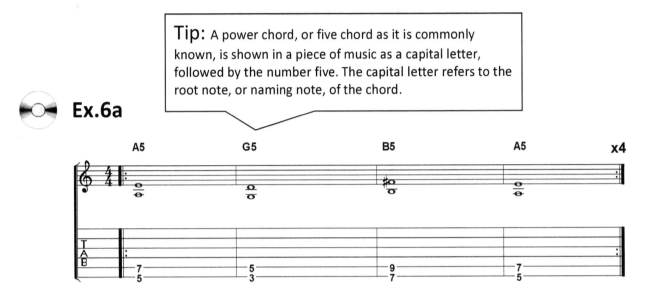

Tip: A power chord, or five chord as it is commonly known, is shown in a piece of music as a capital letter, followed by the number five. The capital letter refers to the root note, or naming note, of the chord.

Ex.6a

Ex.6b

Technique Focus

✓ Be sure to use the tip of your finger, pressing firmly behind the fret wire

✓ Take care to only strum the two fretted strings

Power Chords Song One

The following song is a garage rock piece in the style of The White Stripes and uses 6th string power chords.

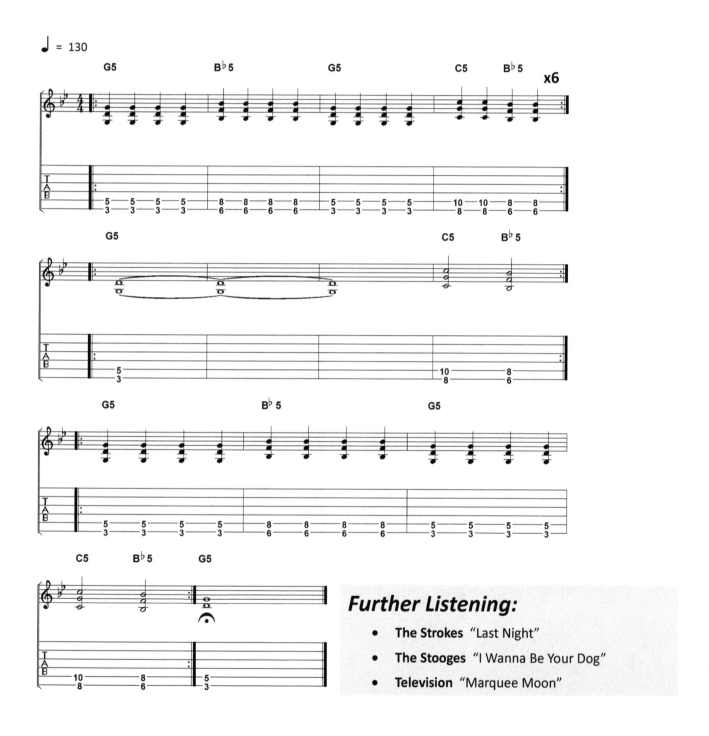

Further Listening:
- **The Strokes** "Last Night"
- **The Stooges** "I Wanna Be Your Dog"
- **Television** "Marquee Moon"

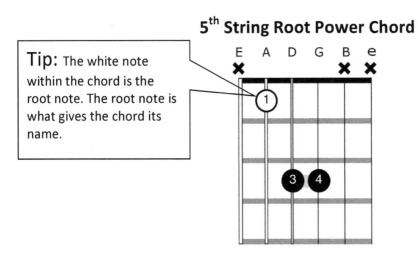

Notes Along the A String

The diagram below shows the notes along the length of the A string. To play a particular chord we need to ensure that the root note is in the correct fret, e.g. for a C5 power chord place the root note at the third fret.

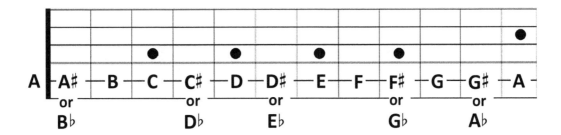

The exercises below utilize the 5th string rootpower chords along the neck.

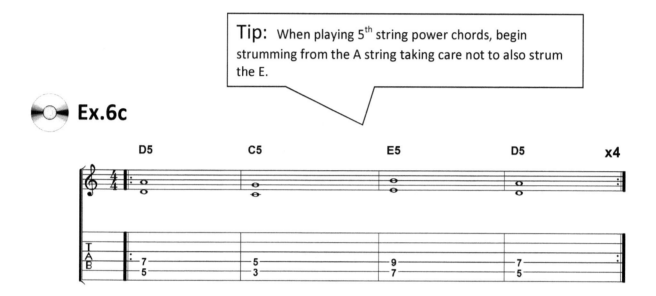

Tip: When playing 5th string power chords, begin strumming from the A string taking care not to also strum the E.

Ex.6c

| D5 | C5 | E5 | D5 | x4 |

```
T|--7---|--5---|--9---|--7---||
A|--5---|--3---|--7---|--5---||
B|------|------|------|------||
```

Ex.6d

| D#5 | C#5 | F#5 | D#5 | x4 |

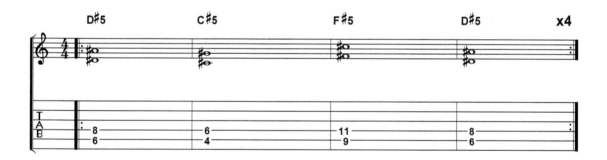

```
T|--8---|--6---|--11--|--8---||
A|--6---|--4---|--9---|--6---||
B|------|------|------|------||
```

Power Chords Song Two

The following song is a punk rock piece in the style of The Offspring.

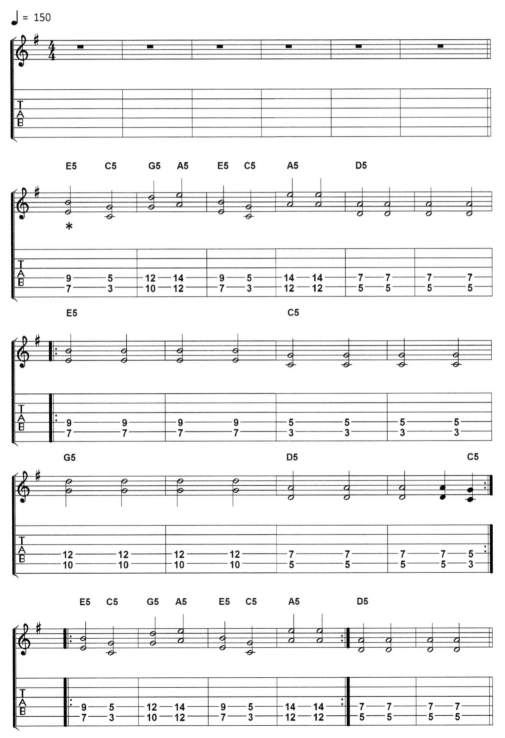

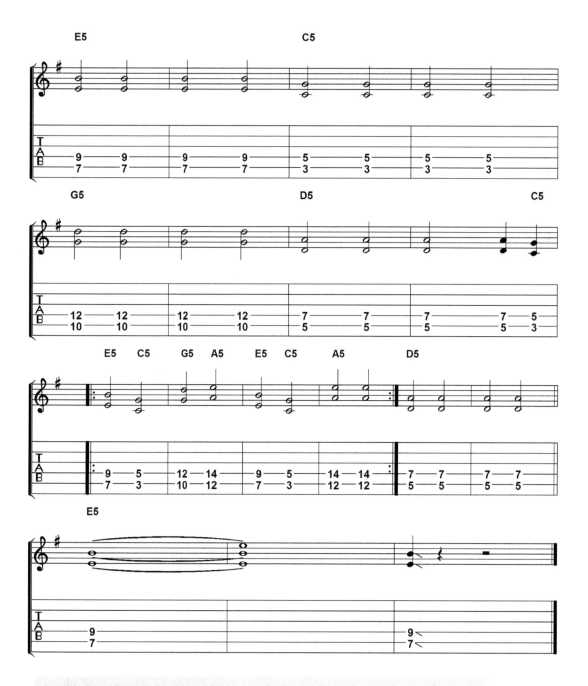

Further Listening:

- **The Ramones** "Sheena Is a Punk Rocker"
- **The Buzzcocks** "Ever Fallen In Love"
- **Green Day** "Basket Case"

Tip: Once this song has been mastered, try playing the piece using an eighth note rhythm, which is found in most punk rock pieces.

An alternative approach to playing power chords is to use three fingers, giving the chord a fuller sound. This approach to playing power chords will also help bridge the gap from playing power chords to barre chords (which will be covered in the next chapter).

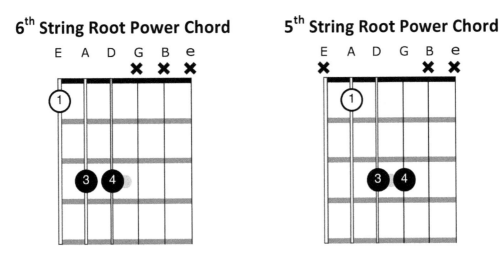

6th and 5th string power chords are often combined in songs to make chord changes quicker and more fluent, as demonstrated below.

Ex.6e

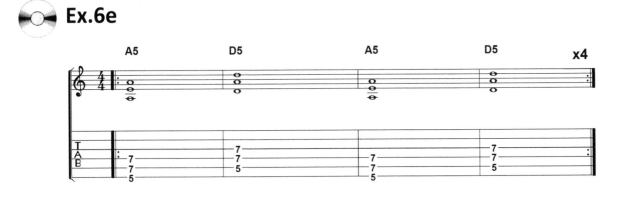

Ex.6f

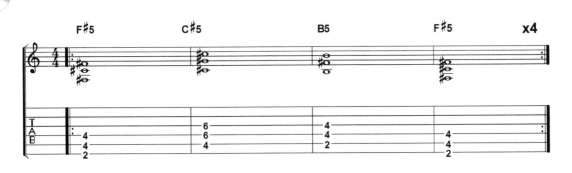

Palm Muting

Palm muting is a common technique and can be found in many different styles of music, from classical to heavy metal. Palm muting is achieved through laying the side/heel of the picking hand across all six strings just in front of the guitar's bridge.

Palm muting is shown in notation as **P.M.**, which is followed by a broken line indicating the section to be palm muted.

 Ex.6g

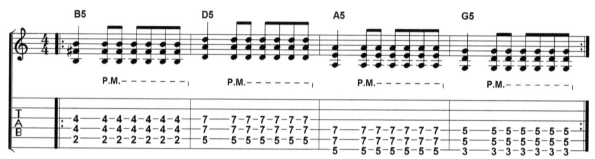

Power Chords Song Three

The last song in this chapter combines both 6th & 5th string power chords along with palm muting in the style of The Foo Fighters.

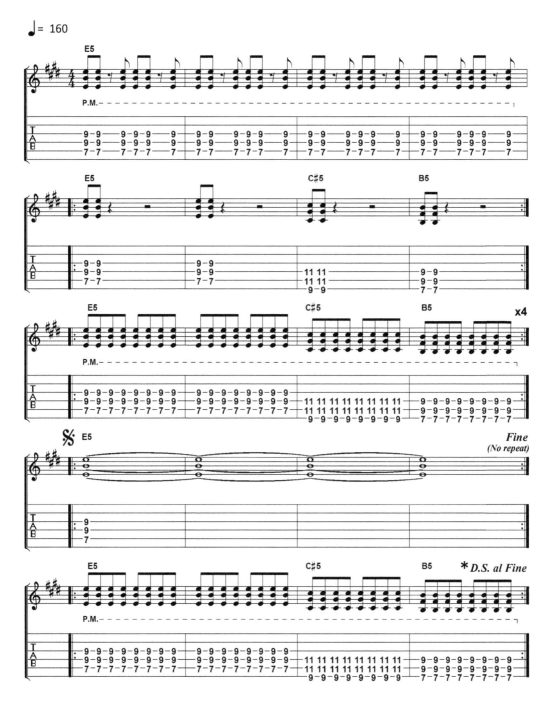

*Tip: This symbol indicates to repeat from the sign (𝄋) and end at **Fine**.

CHAPTER 7   HALF BARRE CHORDS

A half barre chord (sometimes referred to as a partial barre chord) is played using the first finger to fret more than one string at a time, typically two or three strings.

Half Barre chords can be found in many classic Pop & Rock songs such as Plain White T's "Hey There Delilah", Six Pence None The Richer "Kiss Me", Counting Crows "Mr Jones" and Van Halen "Ain't Talkin 'Bout Love".

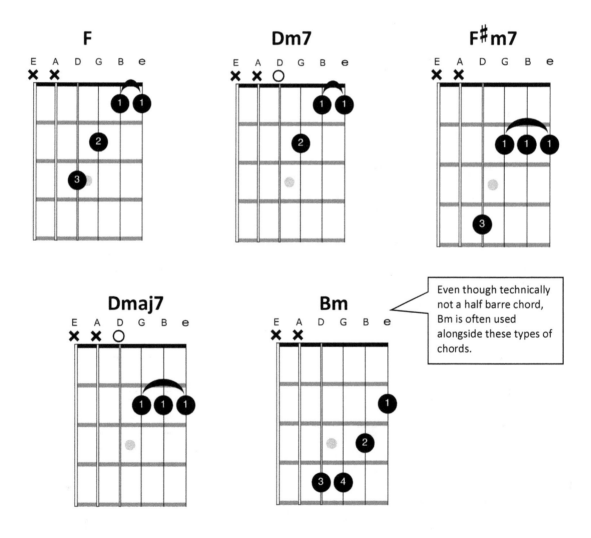

Even though technically not a half barre chord, Bm is often used alongside these types of chords.

Technique Focus

- ✓ Index finger should be parallel with the fret wire
- ✓ Keep remaining fingers arched while using fingertips
- ✓ Ensure the pad of the thumb is in the middle of the neck helping to apply pressure

Ex.7a   F

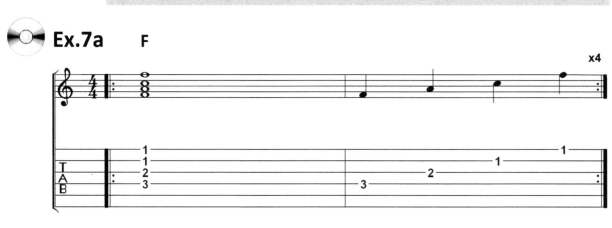

Ex.7b   Dm7

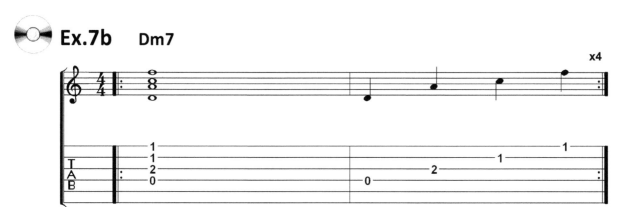

Ex.7c   F#m7

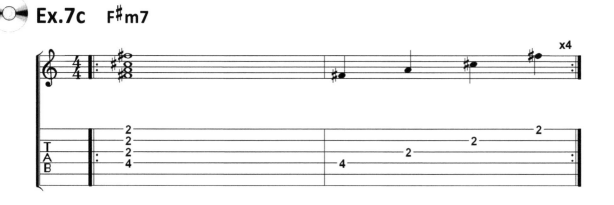

Ex.7d Dmaj7

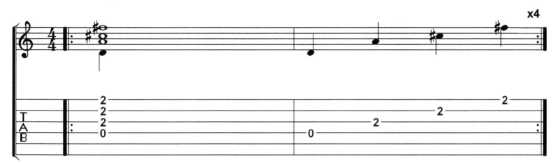

Ex.7e Bm

Half Barre Chords Song One

This song is an americana piece in the style of Counting Crows.

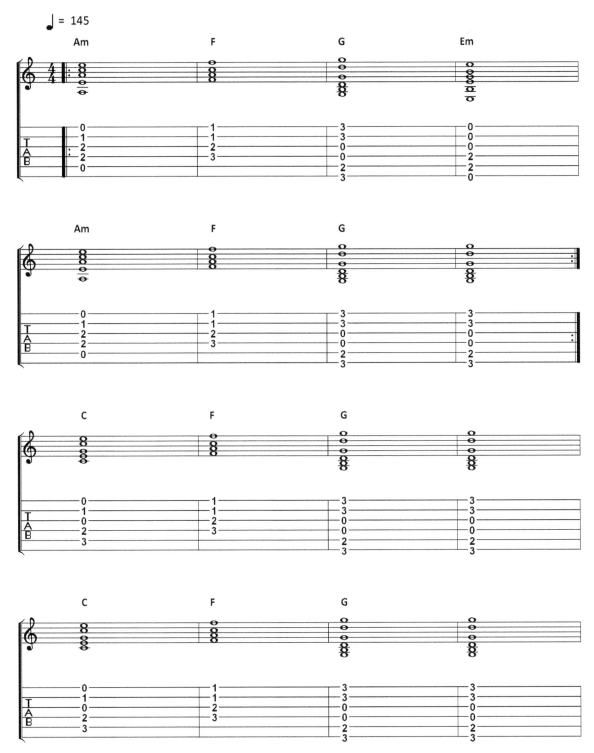

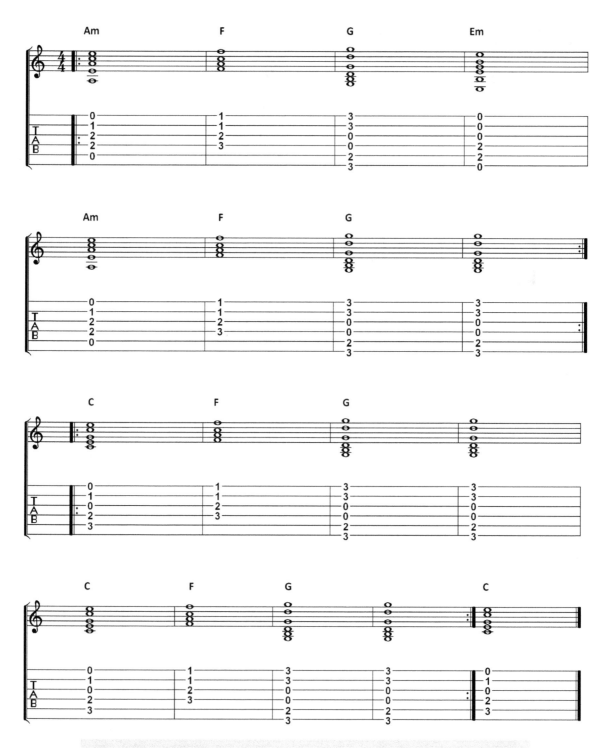

Further Listening:

- **Counting Crows** "Mr. Jones"
- **R.E.M.** "What's the Frequency Kenneth"
- **Sheryl Crow** "There Goes the Neighborhood"

Half Barre Chords Song Two

This song is a folk piece in the style of Mumford and Sons.

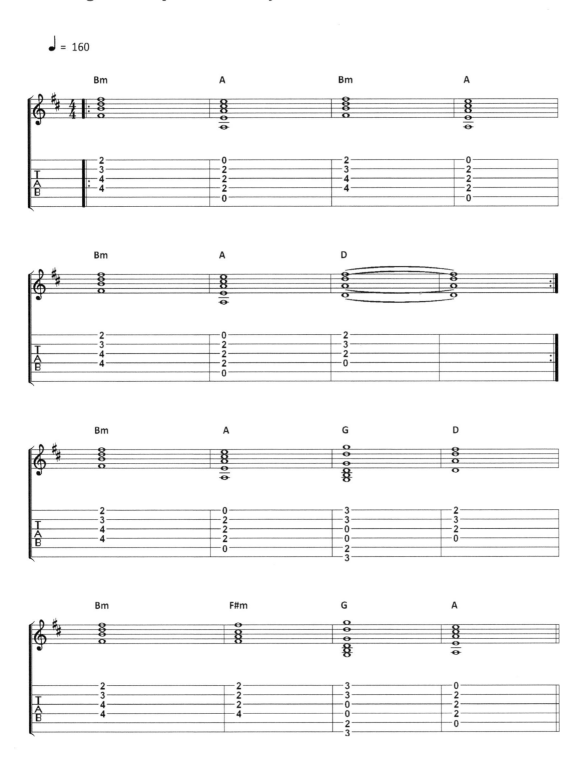

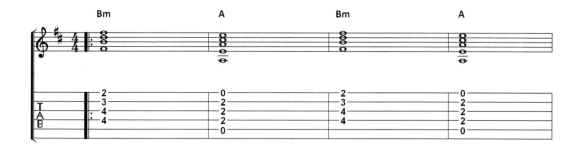

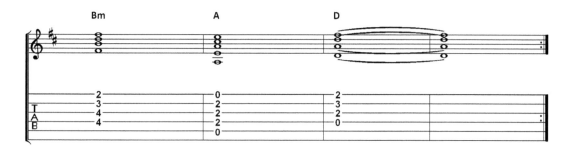

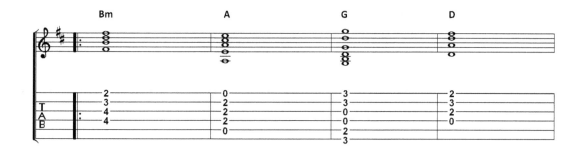

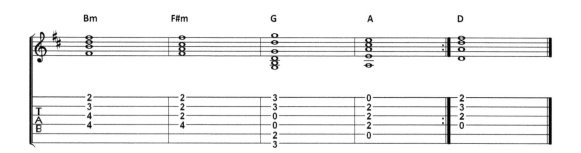

Further Listening:

- **Mumford and Sons** "Little Lion Man"
- **The Lumineers** "Ho Hey"
- **Fleet Foxes** "White Winter Hymnal"

CHAPTER 8   BARRE CHORDS

A barre chord is a closed, movable chord shape that does not contain any open strings. The shape can be moved up and down the neck, which allows you to play in any key without the need to change fingering.

6th String Barre Chords

The chord boxes below show the major and minor barre chord forms with their root notes on the 6th string.

Tip: The curved line above the chord box indicates that the first finger acts as a 'bar' holding down all the strings.

6th String Major Barre Chord

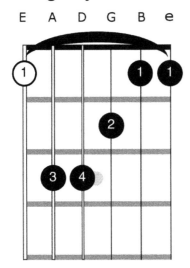

6th String Minor Barre Chord

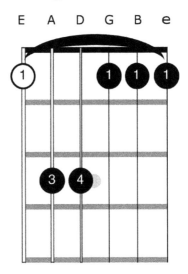

Technique Focus

- ✓ Index finger should be parallel with the fret wire
- ✓ Keep remaining fingers arched while using fingertips
- ✓ Ensure the pad of the thumb is in the middle of the neck helping to apply pressure

Notes Along the Bottom E String

The diagram below shows the notes along the length of the low E string. To play a particular chord we need to ensure that the root note is in the correct fret, e.g. for a G major chord place the root note (finger one) at the third fret.

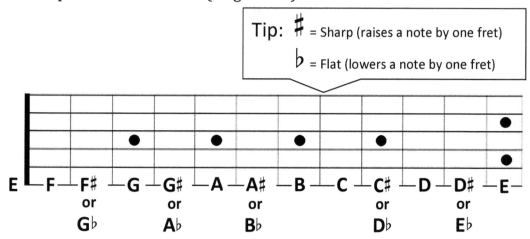

 Ex.8a

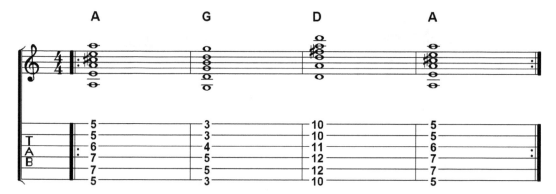

 **Ex.8b**

Barre Chords Song One

The following song is an indie rock piece in the style of The Libertines.

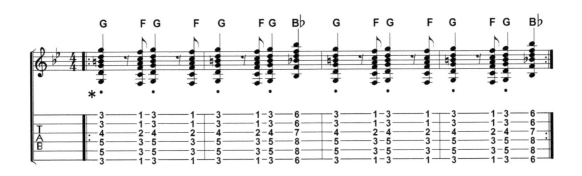

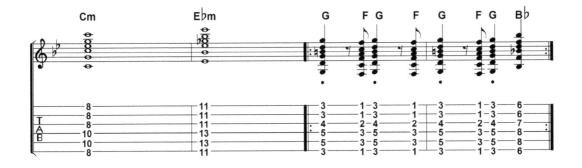

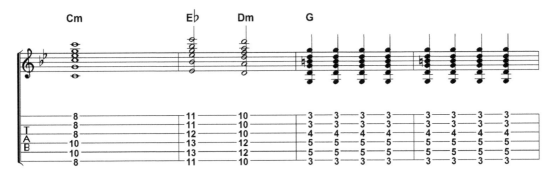

Tip: This symbol (.) indicates Staccato. Staccato is Italian for short or detached and when placed on a note is an instruction to cut the note short by half its length.

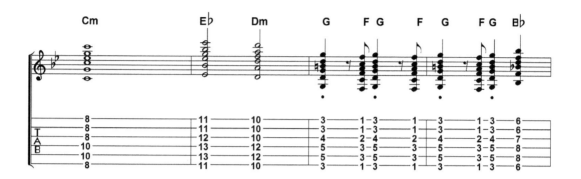

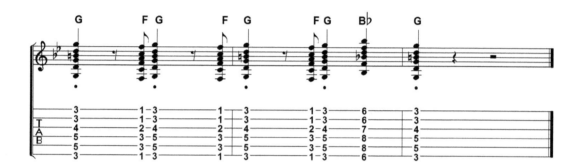

Further Listening:

- **The Undertones** "Teenage Kicks"
- **The Who** "Can't Explain"
- **The Pigeon Detectives** "I Found Out"

5th String Barre Chords

The chord boxes below show the major and minor barre chord forms with their root notes on the 5th string.

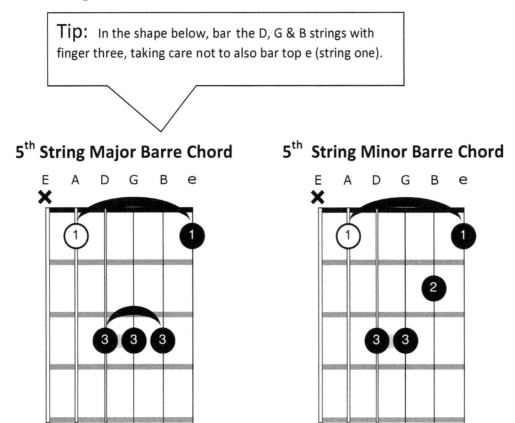

Notes Along the A String

The diagram below shows the notes along the length of the A string. To play a particular chord we need to ensure that the root note is in the correct fret, e.g. for a C major chord place the root note (finger one) at the third fret.

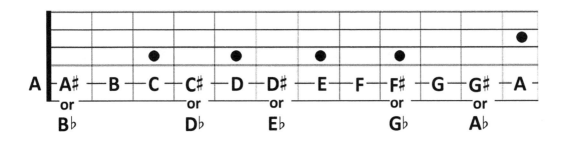

The exercises below utilize both major and minor 5th string barre chords.

 Ex.8c

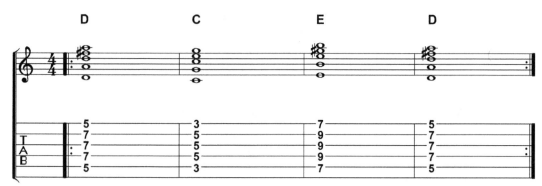

 Ex.8d

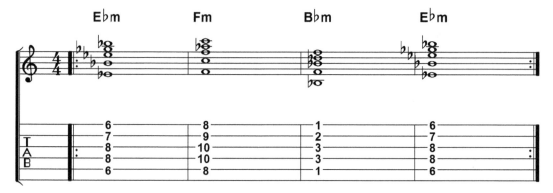

Barre Chords Song Two

The following song is an alternative rock piece in the style of The Fratellis.

Further Listening:

- **The Fratellis** "Whistle For The Choir"
- **Arctic Monkeys** "When The Sun Goes Down"
- **Razorlight** "Golden Touch"

The exercises below combine both 6th and 5th string barre chords.

Ex.8e

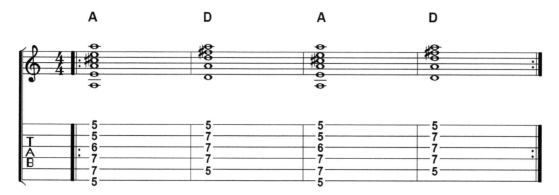

Ex.8f

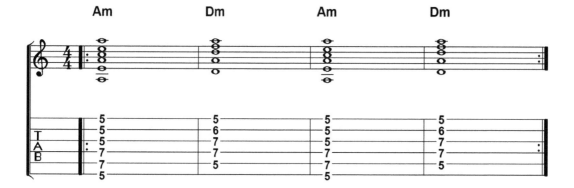

In the following barre chord examples the strings are individually picked rather than strummed; this technique is referred to as an arpeggio.

 Ex.8g

 Ex.8h

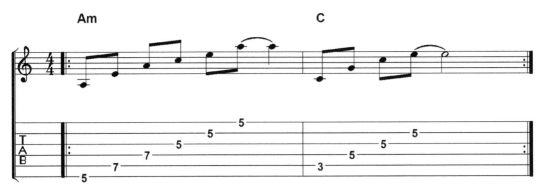

Sixteenth Notes

The sixteenth note lasts for quarter of a beat; this simply means you play four times for each count, as demonstrated below.

When a sixteenth note rhythm is being used in a piece of music it has two lines connecting the notes, whereas an eighth note has one.

Notes	Rests	Name	Value
𝗼	▬	Whole note	4 Counts (one to a bar)
𝅗𝅥	▬	Half note	2 Counts (two to a bar)
♩	𝄽	Quarter note	1 Count (four to a bar)
♪	𝄾	Eighth note	½ Count (eight to a bar)
𝅘𝅥𝅯	𝄿	Sixteenth Notes	¼ Count (sixteen to a bar)

Barre Chords Song Three

The following song is a hip hop piece which utilizes both 6th and 5th string barre chords as well as arpeggios and sixteenth note rhythms.

Further Listening:

- **Robin Thicke** "Lost Without You"
- **TLC** "No Scrubs"
- **Method Man** "Say"

CHAPTER 9   LEAD GUITAR

In the following chapter we will explore the common techniques found in lead guitar such as string bends, hammer-ons, pull-offs and slides. We will also expand our scale knowledge in the process.

Movable Minor Pentatonic Scale

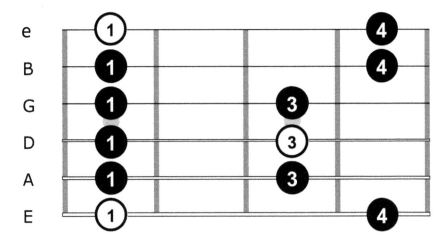

 **Ex.9a**

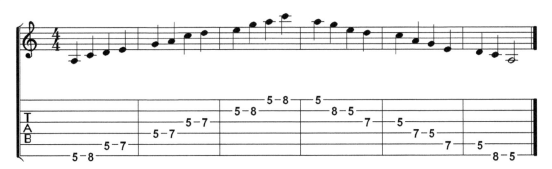

Technique Focus

✓ Start slowly to ensure both hands are coordinated

✓ Keep plectrum at a 45 degree angle

✓ Make sure both hands stay relaxed as tension will result in a loss of flexibility and movement

Alternate Picking

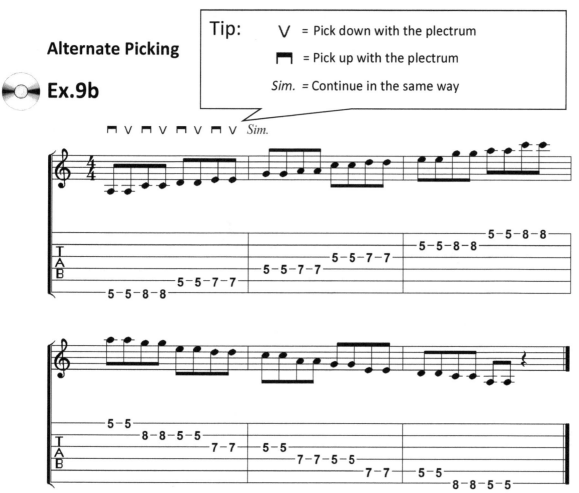

String Bending

String bending is one of the most commonly used techniques in lead guitar and is achieved through pushing a string upward, which raises the pitch of the note by a certain number of frets. There are many different types of string bends, as demonstrated in the table below:

Type	Distance
1½ Tones	3 frets
1 Tone (Full)	2 frets
½ a Tone	1 fret
¼ of a Tone	Bend the string slightly sharp, also referred to as a microtonal bend.

Ex.9c

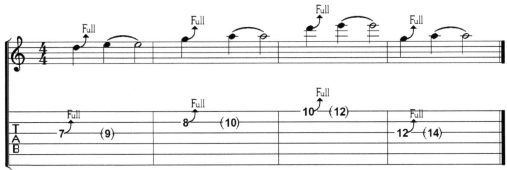

 ### Ex.9d

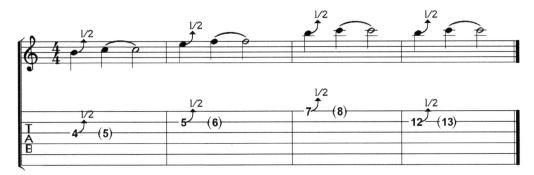

 ### Ex.9e

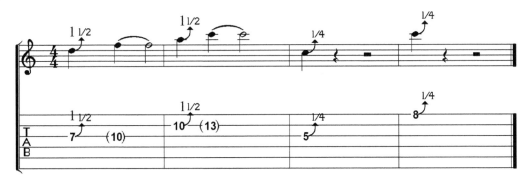

Technique Focus

- ✓ Play the bracketed note in the tab first as this is the target pitch for the bend
- ✓ Use third finger to execute all bends excluding microtonal
- ✓ Use second finger on the same string to add support
- ✓ Use first finger to touch neighbouring strings to help eliminate unwanted noise
- ✓ Hook thumb over the top of the fretboard to form a 'grip' shape as this will give you leverage for the string bend

Hammer-Ons

A hammer-on is shown in the tab as an arched line connecting two different notes; this is an instruction to play the first note as normal but sound the second by 'hammering down' on the string with a fretting-hand finger.

 Ex.9f

 Ex.9g

Technique Focus

- ✓ Use the tip of the finger striking directly behind the fret wire
- ✓ Keep finger close to the string to improve accuracy and control
- ✓ Use sufficient force to produce the same volume as the picked note

Pull-Offs

This particular technique is often combined with a hammer-on, which allows the player to execute fast passages with little effort. When used with distortion it gives a smooth violin/saxophone like sound. 'Pull-off' by pulling the fretting-hand finger off the string at a slight angle to produce the lower note.

 Ex.9h

 Ex.9i

Technique Focus

- ✓ Use the tip of your finger pulling downwards rather than simply lifting your finger straight up off the string
- ✓ Be sure to maintain strength in the lower finger to sound the second note

Slides

The final technique we will look at in this chapter is the slide. Slides are often thought to be related to the Legato family (hammer-ons and pull-offs) as they also produce a smooth sound. Slides can be used with single notes or chords and are a great way for moving or connecting positions on the fretboard.

Slides are indicated in tab by a diagonal line. To perform a slide, keep the note held down and drag it along the fretboard to the desired fret.

Ex.9j

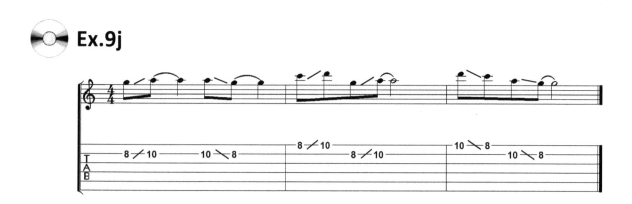

Before moving on to our solo study, here is a lick that combines all the lead guitar techniques covered in this chapter.

Ex.9k

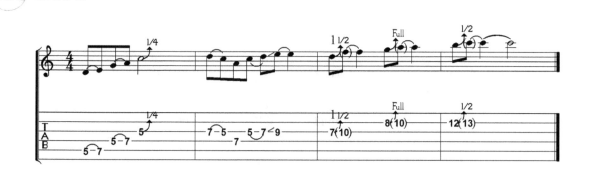

Solo Study

The following song is a rock piece in the style of Pink Floyd's guitarist David Gilmour and includes all of the lead techniques within this chapter.

Further Listening:

- **Pink Floyd** "Comfortably Numb"
- **Jimi Hendrix** "Little Wing"
- **Stevie Ray Vaughan** "Lenny"

LISTENING

Rock	Blues	Metal
AC/DC	Muddy Waters	Van Halen
Aerosmith	Buddy Guy	Black Sabbath
Jimi Hendrix	Otis Rush	Iron Maiden
Led Zeppelin	Stevie Ray Vaughan	Ozzy Osbourne
Pink Floyd	Eric Clapton	Lamb of God
The Eagles	Derek Trucks	Paul Gilbert
The Beatles	Robben Ford	Extreme
The Rolling Stones	B.B. King	Steve Vai
Guns 'N' Roses	Albert King	Joe Satriani
Deep Purple	Freddie King	Yngwie Malmsteen
Santana	T-Bone Walker	Avenged Sevenfold
Dire Straits	Hurbert Sumlin	Metallica
ZZ Top	Albert Collins	Motley Crue
Jeff Beck	John Lee Hooker	Judas Priest
Joe Bonamassa	Peter Green	Bullet For My Valentine
Bon Jovi	Kenny Wayne Sheppard	Pantera

Alternative	Jazz	Country
Nirvana	Charlie Christian	Brad Paisley
Foo Fighters	Wes Montgomery	Brent Mason
U2	Charlie Parker	Chet Atkins
Coldplay	Miles Davis	Albert Lee
REM	Pat Metheny	Merle Travis
Soundgarden	Scott Henderson	Johnny Cash
The Pixies	Mike Stern	Tony Rice
Pearl Jam	John Scofield	Danny Gaton
The Police	Allan Holdsworth	Jerry Donahue
Stone Roses	Pat Martino	Scotty Moore
Smashing Pumpkins	Kenny Burrell	Doc Watson
Jane's Addiction	Jim Hall	James Burton
Red Hot Chili Peppers	Barney Kessel	Johnny Hiland
Oasis	John Mclaughlin	Jimmy Bryant
The White Stripes	Martin Taylor	Don Rich
Blink 182	Frank Gambale	Jerry Reed

LEGEND LEAD GUITAR TECHNIQUES

Hammer-On

Play the first note as normal but sound the second by 'hammering down' on the string with a fretting-hand finger.

Pull-Off

'Pull-off' by pulling the finger off at a slight angle to produce the lower note at the 3rd fret.

String Bend

Push the string upwards until you have reached the desired pitch (shown in brackets).

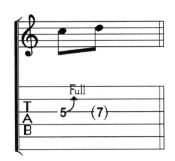

Slide

Play the 3rd fret of the 3rd string; keep an even amount of pressure and 'slide' the note up to the 5th fret.

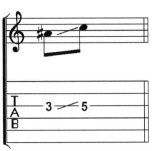

Tapping

Hammer or 'tap' with the middle finger of the picking hand at the 12th fret of the B string and pull-off to the 8th fret.

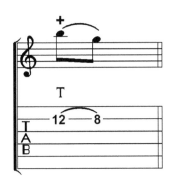

Sweep Picking

Play across the strings using the same consecutive pick stroke.

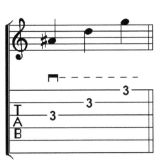

Whammy Bar

Play the open G string and lower or raise the bar to the desired pitch (e.g. -1 = 1fret).

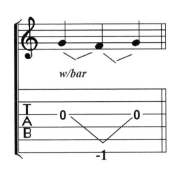

Tremolo Picking

Pick the 3rd fret of the G string as rapidly and continuously as possible.

Rake

Drag the pick across the strings in a single motion.

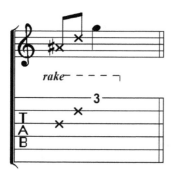

Trills

Rapidly hammer on and pull-off from the 3rd and 5th fret of the G string.

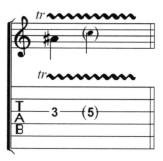

Natural Harmonics

Lightly touch the string directly on the fret wire at the 12th fret of the G string

Pinched Harmonics

Bring the tip of the plectrum level with the side of the thumb. Pick the string at roughly a 40 degree angle.

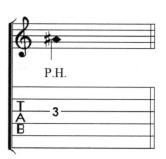

Finger Picking

P = Thumb
I = Index
M = Middle
A = Ring

Plectrum Picking

Pick downwards =

Pick upwards =

General Notation

Treble Clef

The **Treble Clef** is used for high sounding instruments such as Violin, Recorder and Guitar.

Bass Clef

The **Bass Clef** is used for low sounding instruments such as Trombone, Double Bass and Bass Guitar.

Time Signature

The **Time Signature** shows how many beats are in each bar and what note value represents each beat.

Key Signature

The **Key Signature** is a series of sharps or flats that determine the key of a piece of music.

Tempo

The **Tempo** defines the speed of a song in beats per minute.

Sharp

A **Sharp** raises the pitch of a note by a semitone/half step (one fret).

Flat

A **Flat** lowers the pitch of a note by a semitone/half step (one fret).

Natural

A **Natural** cancels out a sharp or flat.

Repeat Marks

Two vertical dots are placed at the start and end of a section, which indicates it is to be repeated.

Would be played: |A|B|C|A|B|C|

1ˢᵗ & 2ⁿᵈ Time Endings

The bar marked **1** is played the first time but omitted on the repeat and replaced with the bar marked **2**.

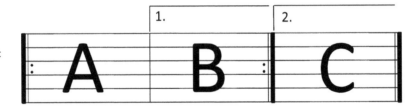

Would be played: |A|B|A|C|

Simile Marks

This symbol indicates to repeat the previous bar.

Would be played: |A|B|B|

Da Capo

Play again from the beginning.

D.C.

Dal Segno

Repeat from the sign (segno).

D.S.

Segno

Symbol used with Dal Segno.

Coda

Indicates to play the section marked with the same symbol.

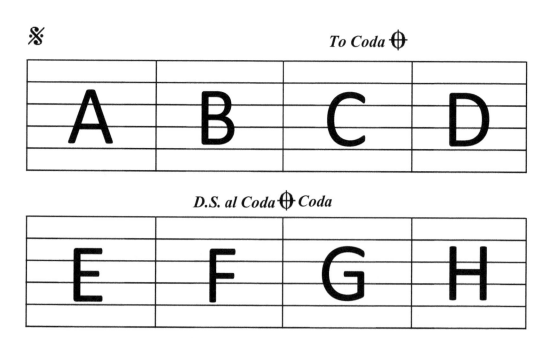

Would be played: |A|B|C|A|B|C|D|

Would be played: |A|B|C|D|E|F|A|B|C|G|H|

— 80 —

Dynamics

Dynamics are used to show changes in volume within a piece of music.

pp   = **Pianissimo** (Very soft)

p   = **Piano** (Soft)

mp   = **Mezzo piano** (Moderately soft)

mf   = **Mezzo forte** (Moderately loud)

f   = **Forte** (Loud)

ff   = **Fortissimo** (Very loud)

<   = **Crescendo** (Gradually getting louder)

>   = **Diminuendo** (Gradually getting softer)

General Musical Terms

Pitch: Is the technical name that refers to the height or depth of a sound.

Interval: The distance between two notes.

Whole Tone: The distance of two frets on the guitar, also referred to as a whole step.

Staccato: Indicates to play notes short and detached, leaving noticeable breaks between notes.

Key: The key is defined by the strongest note or chord in a piece of music. E.g. *"This piece is in 'C' major"* means 'C' is the strongest chord.

Rhythm: Refers to the way in which sounds of different lengths are grouped into patterns.

Semitone: The smallest interval in Western music, the distance of one fret on the guitar, also referred to as a half step.

Legato: Indicates to play in a smooth and even style without leaving breaks between notes.

Bars: A song is divided into bars with each containing a certain number of beats as defined by the time signature, also referred to as measures.

Accompanying Audio

Visit **www.6stringbooks.com/ltpeg** to download the book's accompanying audio.

Please Review

Reviews are gold to authors! If you have enjoyed this book, would you consider rating it and reviewing it on **www.amazon.com?**

Contact Us

Please let us know if you have any questions, suggestions or feedback via **support@6stringbooks.com**

Also Available

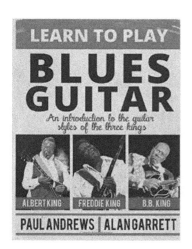

Learn to Play Blues Guitar: An introduction to the guitar styles of the three Kings

"Learn to play the three Kings" delves into the guitar styles of

Albert King, B.B. King and Freddie King.

The book explores the main elements that make up each player's guitar style and is designed to give you the tools and approaches you need to add a little of each style to your own guitar playing.

Available as Paperback and Kindle from

www.amazon.com

CPSIA information can be obtained
at www.ICGtesting.com
Printed in the USA
LVHW021800201218
601239LV00012B/1319